NEW AND SELECTED

POEMS

POEMS

Volume Two

NEW AND SELECTED POEMS

Volume Two

Mary Oliver

BEACON PRESS

BOSTON

Beacon Press
25 Beacon Street
Boston, Massachusetts 02108-2892
www.beacon.org

Beacon Press books
are published under the auspices of
the Unitarian Universalist Association of Congregations.

Text design by Dede Cummings/DCDESIGN

09 08 07 06 05   8 7 6 5 4 3 2 1

This book is printed on acid-free paper that meets the
uncoated paper ANSI/NISO specifications for permanence
as revised in 1992.

Library of Congress Cataloging-in-Publication Data

Oliver, Mary
[Poems.   Selections]
New and selected poems / Mary Oliver
p.   cm.
ISBN 0-8070-6886-1
I. Title
PS3565L7N47   2005
811'.54—DC20   92-7767

Copyright page continues on page 177.

For

Molly Malone Cook

CONTENTS

New Poems

(2004 – 2005)

FROM *Blue Iris*

(2004)

FROM *Why I Wake Early*
(2004)

FROM *Owls and Other Fantasies*
(2003)

FROM *Winter Hours*

(1999)

FROM *West Wind*

(1997)

FROM *White Pine*

(1994)

NEW
POEMS

———— ❦ ————

(2 0 0 4 – 2 0 0 5)

North Country

In the north country now it is spring and there
    is a certain celebration. The thrush
has come home. He is shy and likes the
    evening best, also the hour just before
morning; in that blue and gritty light he
    climbs to his branch, or smoothly
sails there. It is okay to know only
    one song if it is this one. Hear it
rise and fall; the very elements of your soul
    shiver nicely. What would spring be
without it? Mostly frogs. But don't worry, he

arrives, year after year, humble and obedient
    and gorgeous. You listen and you know
you could live a better life than you do, be
    softer, kinder. And maybe this year you will
be able to do it. Hear how his voice
    rises and falls. There is no way to be
sufficiently grateful for the gifts we are
    given, no way to speak the Lord's name
often enough, though we do try, and

especially now, as that dappled breast
    breathes in the pines and heaven's
windows in the north country, now spring has come,
    are opened wide.

Everything

I want to make poems that say right out, plainly,
    what I mean, that don't go looking for the
laces of elaboration, puffed sleeves. I want to
    keep close and use often words like
heavy, heart, joy, soon, and to cherish
    the question mark and her bold sister

the dash. I want to write with quiet hands. I
    want to write while crossing the fields that are
fresh with daisies and everlasting and the
    ordinary grass. I want to make poems while thinking of
the bread of heaven and the
    cup of astonishment; let them be

songs in which nothing is neglected,
    not a hope, not a promise. I want to make poems
that look into the earth and the heavens
    and see the unseeable. I want them to honor
both the heart of faith, and the light of the world;
    the gladness that says, without any words, *everything*.

Children, It's Spring

And this is the lady
whom everyone loves,
Ms. Violet
in her purple gown

or, on special occasions,
a dress the color
of sunlight. She sits
in the mossy weeds and waits

to be noticed.
She loves dampness.
She loves attention.
She loves especially

to be picked by careful fingers,
young fingers, entranced
by what has happened
to the world.

We, the older ones,
call it Spring,
and we have been through it
many times.

But there is still nothing
like the children bringing home
such happiness
in their small hands.

Work, Sometimes

I was sad all day, and why not. There I was, books piled on both sides of the table, paper stacked up, words falling off my tongue.

The robins had been a long time singing, and now it was beginning to rain.

What are we sure of? Happiness isn't a town on a map, or an early arrival, or a job well done, but good work ongoing. Which is not likely to be the trifling around with a poem.

Then it began raining hard, and the flowers in the yard were full of lively fragrance.

You have had days like this, no doubt. And wasn't it wonderful, finally, to leave the room? Ah, what a moment!

As for myself, I swung the door open. And there was the wordless, singing world. And I ran for my life.

Hum

What is this dark hum among the roses?
   The bees have gone simple, sipping,
that's all. What did you expect? Sophistication?
   They're small creatures and they are
filling their bodies with sweetness, how could they not
   moan in happiness? The little
worker bee lives, I have read, about three weeks.
   Is that long? Long enough, I suppose, to understand
that life is a blessing. I have found them—haven't you?—
   stopped in the very cups of the flowers, their wings
a little tattered—so much flying about, to the hive,
   then out into the world, then back, and perhaps dancing,
should the task be to be a scout—sweet, dancing bee.
   I think there isn't anything in this world I don't
admire. If there is, I don't know what it is. I
   haven't met it yet. Nor expect to. The bee is small,
and since I wear glasses, so I can see the traffic and
   read books, I have to
take them off and bend close to study and
   understand what is happening. It's not hard, it's in fact
as instructive as anything I have ever studied. Plus, too,
   it's love almost too fierce to endure, the bee
nuzzling like that into the blouse
   of the rose. And the fragrance, and the honey, and of course
the sun, the purely pure sun, shining, all the while, over
   all of us.

First Happenings

A morning-glory morning with its usual glory,
dawn particularly startling with citrons and
mauves, petunias in the garden flashing their
tender signals of gratitude. The sunflowers
creak in their grass-colored dresses. Cosmos,
the four o'clocks, the sweet alyssum nod to
the roses who so very politely nod back.

And now it is time to go to work. At my desk
I look out over the fluttering petals, little
fires. Each one fresh and almost but not quite
replicable.

Consider wearing such a satisfying body!
Consider being, with your entire self, such
a quiet prayer!

Mysteries, Four of the Simple Ones

How does the seed-grain feel
when it is just beginning to be wheat?

And how does the catbird feel
when the blue eggs break and become little catbirds,

maybe on midsummer night's eve,
and without fanfare?

And how does the turtle feel as she covers her eggs
with the sweep of her feet,
then leaves them for the world to take care of?

Does she know her accomplishment?

And when the blue heron, beaking his long breast feathers,
sees one feather fall, does he know I will find it?
Will he see me holding it in my hand

as he opens his wings
softly and without a sound—
as he rises and floats over the water?

And this is just any day at the edge of the pond,
a black and leafy pond without a name
until I named it.

And what else can we do when the mysteries present themselves

but hope to pluck from the basket the brisk words
that will applaud them,

the heron, the turtle, the catbird, the seed-grain
kneeling in the dark earth, its body
opening into the golden world?

Holding Benjamin

No use to tell him
that he

and the raccoon are brothers.
You have your soft ideas about nature,

he has others,
and they are full of his

white teeth
and lip that curls, sometimes,

horribly.
You love

this earnest dog,
but also you admire the raccoon

and Lord help you in your place
of hope and improbables.

To the black-masked gray one:
Run! you say,

and just as urgently, to the dog:
Stay!

and he won't or he will,
depending

on more things than I could name.
He's sure he's right

and you, so tangled in your mind,
are wrong,

though patient and pacific.
And you are downcast.

And it's his eyes, not yours,
that are clear and bright.

White Heron Rises Over Blackwater

I wonder
  what it is
    that I will accomplish
     today

if anything
  can be called
    that marvelous word.
     It won't be

my kind of work,
  which is only putting
    words on a page,
     the pencil

haltingly calling up
  the light of the world,
    yet nothing appearing on paper
     half as bright

as the mockingbird's
  verbal hilarity
    in the still unleafed shrub
     in the churchyard—

or the white heron
  rising
    over the swamp
     and the darkness,

his yellow eyes
   and broad wings wearing
      the light of the world
      in the light of the world—

ah yes, I see him.
   He is exactly
      the poem
         I wanted to write.

The Real Prayers Are Not the Words, but the Attention that Comes First

The little hawk leaned sideways and, tilted, rode the wind. Its eye at this distance looked like green glass; its feet were the color of butter. Speed, obviously, was joy. But then, so was the sudden, slow circle it carved into the slightly silvery air, and the squaring of its shoulders, and the pulling into itself the long, sharp-edged wings, and the fall into the grass where it tussled a moment, like a bundle of brown leaves, and then, again, lifted itself into the air, that butter-color clenched in order to hold a small, still body, and it flew off as my mind sang out oh all that loose, blue rink of sky, where does it go to, and why?

Black Bear in the Orchard

It was a long winter.
   But the bees were mostly awake
in their perfect house,
   the workers whirling their wings
to make heat.
   Then the bear woke,

too hungry not to remember
   where the orchard was,
and the hives.
   He was not a picklock.
He was a sledge that leaned
   into their front wall and came out

the other side.
   What could the bees do?
Their stings were as nothing.
   They had planned everything
sufficiently
   except for this: catastrophe.

They slumped under the bear's breath.
   They vanished into the curl of his tongue.
Some had just enough time
   to think of how it might have been—
the cold easing,
   the smell of leaves and flowers

floating in,
    then the scouts going out,
then their coming back, and their dancing—
    nothing different
but what happens in our own village.
    What pity for the tiny souls

who are so hopeful, and work so diligently
    until time brings, as it does, the slap and the claw.
Someday, of course, the bear himself
    will become a bee, a honey bee, in the general mixing.
Nature, under her long green hair,
    has such unbendable rules,

and a bee is not a powerful thing, even
    when there are many,
as people, in a town or a village.
    And what, moreover, is catastrophe?
Is it the sharp sword of God,
    or just some other wild body, loving its life?

Not caring a whit, black bear
    blinks his horrible, beautiful eyes,
slicks his teeth with his fat and happy tongue,
    and saunters on.

Honey Locust

Who can tell how lovely in June is the
    honey locust tree, or why
a tree should be so sweet and live
    in this world? Each white blossom
on a dangle of white flowers holds one green seed—
    a new life. Also each blossom on a dangle of flowers
        holds a flask
of fragrance called *Heaven,* which is never sealed.
    The bees circle the tree and dive into it. They are crazy
with gratitude. They are working like farmers. They are as
    happy as saints. After awhile the flowers begin to
wilt and drop down into the grass. Welcome
    shines in the grass.

                     Every year I gather
handfuls of blossoms and eat of their mealiness; the honey
    melts in my mouth, the seeds make me strong,
both when they are crisp and ripe, and even at the end
    when their petals have turned dull yellow.

                            So it is
if the heart has devoted itself to love, there is
    not a single inch of emptiness. Gladness gleams
all the way to the grave.

Percy (One)

Our new dog, named for the beloved poet,
ate a book which unfortunately we had
    left unguarded.
Fortunately it was the *Bhagavad Gita,*
of which many copies are available.
Every day now, as Percy grows
into the beauty of his life, we touch
his wild, curly head and say,

"Oh, wisest of little dogs."

What Is There Beyond Knowing

What is there beyond knowing that keeps
calling to me? I can't

turn in any direction
but it's there. I don't mean

the leaves' grip and shine or even the thrush's
silk song, but the far-off

fires, for example,
of the stars, heaven's slowly turning

theater of light, or the wind
playful with its breath;

or time that's always rushing forward,
or standing still

in the same—what shall I say—
moment.

What I know
I could put into a pack

as if it were bread and cheese, and carry it
on one shoulder,

important and honorable, but so small!
While everything else continues, unexplained

and unexplainable. How wonderful it is

to follow a thought quietly

to its logical end.
I have done this a few times.

But mostly I just stand in the dark field,
in the middle of the world, breathing

in and out. Life so far doesn't have any other name
but breath and light, wind and rain.

If there's a temple, I haven't found it yet.
I simply go on drifting, in the heaven of the grass
    and the weeds.

Ravens

I don't know what the ravens are saying this
     morning of green tenderness and
rain but, my, what a collection of
     squallings and cracklings and whistles, made

with the ruffling of throat feathers and the
     stretching of wings, nor is it any single speech
one to the rest but, clearly, an octet, since
     they are eight coal-black birds with
dark-brown eyes. I have been in this world just
     long enough to learn (not always easily) to love

my neighbors and to allow them every
     possibility. Maybe the ravens are talking
for some ultimate vicious but useful purpose, or
     maybe it's only directions to the next mountain, or maybe
it's simple, silly joy. "Hello, ravens," I say, under
     their dark tree and, as if courtesy were of

great importance, they turn, they clack and spill their
     delicious glottals, of no consequence but
friendly and without the least judgment, down and
     over me.

The Measure

I stopped the car and ran back and across the road
and picked up the box turtle, who only
hissed and withdrew herself into her pretty shell.
Well, goodness, it was early in the morning, not too much
    traffic.
Rather an adventure than a risk, and anyway
who wouldn't give aid to such a shy citizen?
Who wouldn't complete the journey for it, taking it of course
in the direction of its desire: a pinewoods
where, as I learned, the blueberries ripen early.
Probably she had thought, in the middle of the night—
    Ah, it's time.
Sometimes I think our own lives are watched over like that.
Out of the mystery of the hours and the days
something says—Let's give this one a little trial.
Let's, say, put a turtle in the road she's traveling on, and
    in a hurry.
Let's see how her life is measuring up, that lucky girl.
So much happiness, so much good fortune. Ah, it's time.

Truro, the Blueberry Fields

Not far from where I start to gather the ripened berries
I begin, as usual, to slow down. Then, pretty soon, I am
doing nothing. I am just sitting there in the little bundles
of leaves.

In the distance a sparrow is singing over and over his
serene and very simple song. Oh, to hear him within the
enclosure of nothing else!

Friend, I am becoming desperate. What shall I do? How
quickly, if I only knew by what remedy, I would turn
from the commotion of my own life.

While on and on and on, the sparrow sings.

Oxygen

Everything needs it: bone, muscles, and even,
while it calls the earth its home, the soul.
So the merciful, noisy machine

stands in our house working away in its
lung-like voice. I hear it as I kneel
before the fire, stirring with a

stick of iron, letting the logs
lie more loosely. You, in the upstairs room,
are in your usual position, leaning on your

right shoulder which aches
all day. You are breathing
patiently; it is a

beautiful sound. It is
your life, which is so close
to my own that I would not know

where to drop the knife of
separation. And what does this have to do
with love, except

everything? Now the fire rises
and offers a dozen, singing, deep-red
roses of flame. Then it settles

to quietude, or maybe gratitude, as it feeds
as we all do, as we must, upon the invisible gift:
our purest, sweet necessity: the air.

Climbing Pinnacle

It is only a small mountain
   as mountains go,
too stubby for any map.
   But still, in my boots,

I climbed and climbed
   until at last there was nothing
but the blue sky
   and a single final pasture

and a few not-very-tall trees—
   and from under these came running
a fawn on its tumbly legs,
   the sound of its wanting falling
from its pink, pursed mouth.
   But I knew the rule:

Don't touch it, or the doe
   might never come back!
So what could I do? It almost
   reached me
before I slung myself into a tree.
   And there I was,

higher even than the mountain,
   perched for hours
while beauty held me tightly
   with the long lashes of its dark eyes
and the delicate, stamping hooves.
   Below me I could see and hear

the tiny people calling my name
    in the far-below fields—
even the great horse, Jack,
    was sniffing among the grasses.
But I didn't move
    until the doe came back,

angry and snorting,
    and she and the fawn tiptoed away.
And so I was free.
    And there was nothing to do,
as there is never anything to do,
    after rapture,

but to swing down
    bough after bough—
to hurry down, field after field,
    through the pale twilight,
to be greeted by the people
    who loved me, far below.

Mountain Lion on East Hill Road, Austerlitz, N.Y.

Once, years ago, I saw
   the mountain cat. She stepped
     from under a cloud
       of birch trees and padded

along the edge of the field. When she saw
   that I saw her, instantly
     flames leaped
       in her eyes, it was that

distasteful to her to be
   seen. Her wide face
     was a plate of gold,
       her black lip

curled as though she had come
   to a terrible place in the long movie, her shoulders
     shook like water, her tail
       swung at the grass

as she turned back under the trees,
   just leaving me time to guess
     that she was not a cat at all
       but a lean and perfect mystery

that perhaps I didn't really see,
   but simply understood belonged here
     like all the other perfections
       that still, occasionally, emerge

out of the last waterfalls, forests,
   the last unviolated mountains, hurrying
    day after day, year after year
      through the cage of the world.

Circles

In the morning the blue heron is busy
    stepping, slowly, around the edge of the
pond. He is tall and shining. His wings, folded
    against his body, fit so neatly they
make of him, when he lifts his shoulders and begins to rise
    into the air, a great surprise. Also
he carries so lightly the terrible sword-beak. Then
    he is gone over the trees.

        I am so happy to be alive in this world
I would like to live forever, but I am
    content not to. Seeing what I have seen
has filled me; believing what I believe
    has filled me.

        The first words of this page are
hardly thought of when the bird
    circles back over the trees; it floats down
like an armful of blue flowers, a bundle of light
    coming to refresh itself again in the black water, and I think:
maybe it is or it isn't the same bird—maybe it's
    the first one's child, or the child of its child.
What I mean is, our deliverance from Time
    and the continuance, if we only steward them well,
of earthly things. So maybe it's myself still standing here, or
    someone else, like myself hot with the joy of this world, and
filled with praise.

Tiger Lilies

They blew in the wind softly, this way,
that way. They were not disappointed
when they saw the scissors, rather they
braced themselves sweetly and shone
with willingness. They were on tall and
tender poles, with wheels of leaves.
They were soft as the ears of kittens.
They felt warm in recognition of the
summer day. A dozen was plenty. I held
them in my arms. They were silent the
way the deepest water is silent. If they
wondered where they were going they
didn't show it, as they sprinkled freely
over my shirt and my hands their
precious gold dust.

Of What Surrounds Me

Whatever it is I am saying, I always
    need a leaf or a flower, if not an
entire field. As for sky, I am so wildly
    in love with each day's inventions, cool blue
or cat gray or full
    of the ships of clouds, I simply can't
say whatever it is I am saying without
    at least one skyful. That leaves water, a
creek or a well, river or ocean, it has to be
    there. For the heart to be there. For the pen
to be poised. For the idea to come.

The Faces of Deer

When for too long I don't go deep enough into the woods to see them, they begin to enter my dreams. Yes, there they are, in the pinewoods of my inner life. I want to live a life full of modesty and praise. Each hoof of each animal makes the sign of a heart as it touches then lifts away from the ground. Unless you believe that heaven is very near, how will you find it? Their eyes are pools in which one would be content, on any summer afternoon, to swim away through the door of the world. Then, love and its blessing. Then: heaven.

Terns

Don't think just now of the trudging forward of thought,
but of the wing-drive of unquestioning affirmation.

It's summer, you never saw such a blue sky,
and here they are, those white birds with quick wings,

sweeping over the waves,
chattering and plunging,

their thin beaks snapping, their hard eyes
happy as little nails.

The years to come—this is a promise—
will grant you ample time

to try the difficult steps in the empire of thought
where you seek for the shining proofs you think you must have.

But nothing you ever understand will be sweeter, or more binding,
than this deepest affinity between your eyes and the world.

The flock thickens
over the roiling, salt brightness. Listen,

maybe such devotion, in which one holds the world
in the clasp of attention, isn't the perfect prayer,

but it must be close, for the sorrow, whose name is doubt,
is thus subdued, and not through the weaponry of reason,

but of pure submission. Tell me, what else
could beauty be for? And now the tide

is at its very crown,
the white birds sprinkle down,

gathering up the loose silver, rising
as if weightless. It isn't instruction, or a parable.

It isn't for any vanity or ambition
except for the one allowed, to stay alive.

It's only a nimble frolic
over the waves. And you find, for hours,

you cannot even remember the questions
that weigh so in your mind.

Wild, Wild

This is what love is:
the dry rose bush the gardener, in his pruning, missed
suddenly bursts into bloom.
A madness of delight; an obsession.
A holy gift, certainly.
But often, alas, improbable.

Why couldn't Romeo have settled for someone else?
Why couldn't Tristan and Isolde have refused
the shining cup
which would have left peaceful the whole kingdom?

Wild sings the bird of the heart in the forests
    of our lives.

Over and over Faust, standing in the garden, doesn't know
anything that's going to happen, he only sees
    the face of Marguerite, which is irresistible.

And wild, wild sings the bird.

The Poet With His Face in His Hands

You want to cry aloud for your
mistakes. But to tell the truth the world
doesn't need any more of that sound.

So if you're going to do it and can't
stop yourself, if your pretty mouth can't
hold it in, at least go by yourself across

the forty fields and the forty dark inclines
of rocks and water to the place where
the falls are flinging out their white sheets

like crazy, and there is a cave behind all that
jubilation and water-fun and you can
stand there, under it, and roar all you

want and nothing will be disturbed; you can
drip with despair all afternoon and still,
on a green branch, its wings just lightly touched

by the passing foil of the water, the thrush,
puffing out its spotted breast, will sing
of the perfect, stone-hard beauty of everything.

Over the Hill She Came

Over the hill
   she came,
      her long legs
         very scarcely

touching the ground,
   the cups of her ears
      listening,
         with obvious pleasure,

to the wind
   as it stroked
      the dark arms
         of the pines;

once or twice
   she lingered
      and browsed
         some moist patch

of half-wrapped leaves,
   then came along
      to where I was—
         or nearly—

and then, among the thousand bodies
   of the trees,
      their splashes of light and their shadows,
         she was gone;

and I, who was heavy that day
   with thoughts as small as my whole life
      would ever be,
         and especially

compared to the thousand shining trees,
   gave thanks to whatever sent her
      in my direction
         that I might see, and strive to be,

as clearly she was,
   beyond sorrow,
      careless, soft-lipped angel
         walking on air.

Reckless Poem

Today again I am hardly myself.
It happens over and over.
It is heaven-sent.

It flows through me
like the blue wave.
Green leaves—you may believe this or not—
have once or twice
burst from the tips of my fingers

somewhere
deep in the woods,
in the reckless seizure of spring.

Though, of course, I also know that other song,
the sweet passion of one-ness.

Just yesterday I watched an ant crossing a path, through the
    tumbled pine needles she toiled.
And I thought: she will never live another life but this one.
And I thought: if she lives her life with all her strength
    is she not wonderful and wise?
And I continued this up the miraculous pyramid of everything
    until I came to myself.

And still, even in these northern woods, on these hills of sand
I have flown from the window of myself

to become white heron, gray whale,
    fox, hedgehog, camel.
Oh, sometimes already my body has felt like the body of a flower!
Sometimes already my heart is a red parrot, perched
among strange, dark trees, flapping and screaming.

The Book

Lilies—as tall as ourselves and more lovely,
　　and full of fragrance, and long orange tongues,
　　　　and those playthings the bees—stood in

a neighbor's yard, a thick, ramping
　　hedge of them. You could not help but see
　　　　that to be beautiful is also to be simple

and brief; is to rise up and be glorious, and then vanish;
　　is to be silent but as though a song was in you only it
　　　　hasn't yet been heard

at least in a garden of real earth and sparrows and wrens,
　　and people hurrying by, pausing then hurrying on
　　　　to the usual daily foolishness that comes to so little

so far as the real things matter: eternity,
　　the unseen, the unrecognized, the filling of the heart
　　　　with goodness, as if it were a hive

in which nothing corrupt could live. And I thought
　　if any one of them could write
　　　　the story of their lives, who wouldn't

stand in line and hand over the last of their
　　shining money—oh, the very end of their shining money—
　　　　to buy it.

Meanwhile

Lord, my body is not yet a temple,
    but only one of your fair fields.
    An empty field that nobody wants, at least not yet.
    But even here the lily is somewhere.
    Sometimes it lifts its head above the grasses,
    the daisies, the milkweed, the mallow.

And sometimes, like us, it sleeps, or at least
    leans below the blades of the grasses.
    Lord, I live as you have made me to live.
    I bite hungrily into the peach and the turnip.
    I bite, with sorrow, into the calf and the lamb.
    I drink the tears of the clouds.

I praise the leaves of the shrub oaks
    and the pine trees in their bold coats.
    I listen and give thanks to the catbird and the thrush.
    Meanwhile, the fox knows where you are.
    The bees leave the swamp azalea and fly straight
    to the shadow of your face.

Meanwhile my body is rustic and brash.
    The world I live in is hedges, and small blossoms.
    Lord, consider me, and my earnest work.
    A hut I have made, out of the grasses.
    Now I build the door, out of all things brash and rustic.
    Day and night it is open.
    Have you seen it yet, among the grasses?

    How it longs for you?
    How it tries to shine, like gold?

Song for Autumn

In the deep fall
     don't you imagine the leaves think how
comfortable it will be to touch
     the earth instead of the
nothingness of air and the endless
     freshets of wind? And don't you think
the trees themselves, especially those with mossy,
     warm caves, begin to think

of the birds that will come—six, a dozen—to sleep
     inside their bodies? And don't you hear
the goldenrod whispering goodbye,
     the everlasting being crowned with the first
tuffets of snow? The pond
     vanishes, and the white field over which
the fox runs so quickly brings out
     its blue shadows. And the wind pumps its
bellows. And at evening especially,
     the piled firewood shifts a little,
longing to be on its way.

In Praise of Craziness, of a Certain Kind

On cold evenings
my grandmother,
with ownership of half her mind—
the other half having flown back to Bohemia—

spread newspapers over the porch floor
so, she said, the garden ants could crawl beneath,
as under a blanket, and keep warm,

and what shall I wish for, for myself,
but, being so struck by the lightning of years,
to be like her with what is left, that loving.

Patience

What is the good life now? Why,
look here, consider
the moon's white crescent

rounding, slowly, over
the half month to still another
perfect circle—

the shining eye
that lightens the hills,
that lays down the shadows

of the branches of the trees,
that summons the flowers
to open their sleepy faces and look up

into the heavens.
I used to hurry everywhere,
and leaped over the running creeks.

There wasn't
time enough for all the wonderful things
I could think of to do

in a single day. Patience
comes to the bones
before it takes root in the heart

as another good idea.
I say this
as I stand in the woods

and study the patterns
of the moon shadows,
or stroll down into the waters

that now, late summer, have also
caught the fever, and hardly move
from one eternity to another.

Percy (Two)

I have a little dog who likes to nap with me.
He climbs on my body and puts his face in my neck.
He is sweeter than soap.
He is more wonderful than a diamond necklace,
    which can't even bark.
I would like to take him to Kashmir and the Ukraine,
    and Jerusalem and Palestine and Iraq and Darfur,
that the sorrowing thousands might see his laughing mouth.
I would like to take him to Washington, right into
    the oval office
where Donald Rumsfeld would crawl out of the president's
    armpit
and kneel down on the carpet, and romp like a boy.

For once, for a moment, a rational man.

What the Body Says

I was born here, and
I belong here, and
I will never leave.
The blue heron's

gray smoke will flow over me
for years
and the wind will decide
all directions

until I am safely and entirely
something else.
I am thinking of this
this winter morning

as I sit by the fire
and the fire in its red rack
keeps singing
its crackling song

of transformation.
Of course
I wonder about
the mystery

that is surely up there
in starry space
and how some part of me
will go there at last.

But I am talking now
of the way the body speaks,
and the wind, that keeps saying,
firmly, lovingly:

a little while and then this body
will be stone; then
it will be water; then
it will be air.

Fireflies

At Blackwater
fireflies
are not even a dime a dozen—
they are free,

and each floats and turns
among the branches of the oaks
and the swamp azaleas
looking for another

as, who doesn't?
Oh, blessings
on the intimacy
inside fruition,

be it foxes
or the fireflies
or the dampness inside the petals
of a thousand flowers.

Though Eden is lost
its loveliness
remains in the heart
and the imagination;

he would take her
in a boat
over the dark water;
she would take him

to an island she knows
where the blue flag grows wild
and the grass is deep,
where the birds

perch together,
feather to feather,
on the bough.
And the fireflies,

blinking their little lights,
hurry toward one another.
And the world continues,
God willing.

The Owl Who Comes

The owl who comes
through the dark
to sit
in the black boughs of the apple tree

and stare down
the hook of his beak,
dead silent,
and his eyes,

like two moons
in the distance,
soft and shining
under their heavy lashes—

like the most beautiful lie—
is thinking
of nothing
as he watches

and waits to see
what might appear,
briskly,
out of the seamless,

deep winter—
out of the teeming
world below—
and if I wish the owl luck,

and I do,
what am I wishing for that other
soft life,
climbing through the snow?

What we must do,
I suppose,
is to hope the world
keeps its balance;

what we are to do, however,
with our hearts
waiting and watching—truly
I do not know.

Lead

Here is a story
to break your heart.
Are you willing?
This winter
the loons came to our harbor
and died, one by one,
of nothing we could see.
A friend told me
of one on the shore
that lifted its head and opened
the elegant beak and cried out
in the long, sweet savoring of its life
which, if you have heard it,
you know is a sacred thing,
and for which, if you have not heard it,
you had better hurry to where
they still sing.
And, believe me, tell no one
just where that is.
The next morning
this loon, speckled
and iridescent and with a plan
to fly home
to some hidden lake,
was dead on the shore.
I tell you this
to break your heart,
by which I mean only
that it break open and never close again
to the rest of the world.

The Cricket and the Rose

In fall
the cricket
beneath the rose bush
watches

as the roses fall
to the very ground
that is his kingdom also.
So they're neighbors,

one full of fragrance,
the other
the harper
of a single dry song.

We call this time of the year
the beginning of the end
of another circle,
a convenience

and nothing more.
For the cricket's song
is surely a prayer,
and a prayer, when it is given,

is given forever.
This is a truth
I'm sure of,
for I'm older than I used to be,

and therefore I understand things
nobody would think of
who's young and in a hurry.
The snow is very beautiful.

Under it are the lingering
petals of fragrance,
and the timeless body
of prayer.

Little Dog's Rhapsody in the Night (Percy Three)

He puts his cheek against mine
and makes small, expressive sounds.
And when I'm awake, or awake enough

he turns upside down, his four paws
    in the air
and his eyes dark and fervent.

Tell me you love me, he says.

Tell me again.

Could there be a sweeter arrangement? Over and over
he gets to ask it.
I get to tell.

What I Have Learned So Far

Meditation is old and honorable, so why should I
not sit, every morning of my life, on the hillside,
looking into the shining world? Because, proper-
ly attended to, delight, as well as havoc, is sug-
gestion. Can one be passionate about the just, the
ideal, the sublime, and the holy, and yet commit
to no labor in its cause? I don't think so.

All summations have a beginning, all effect has a
story, all kindness begins with the sown seed.
Thought buds toward radiance. The gospel of
light is the crossroads of—indolence, or action.

Be ignited, or be gone.

FROM

Blue Iris

❦

(2 0 0 4)

The Bleeding-heart

I know a bleeding-heart plant that has thrived
for sixty years if not more, and has never
missed a spring without rising and spreading
itself into a glossy bush, with many small red
hearts dangling. Don't you think that deserves
a little thought? The woman who planted it
has been gone for a long time, and everyone
who saw it in that time has also died or moved
away and so, like so many stories, this one can't
get finished properly. Most things that are
important, have you noticed, lack a certain
neatness. More delicious, anyway, is to
remember my grandmother's pleasure when
the dissolve of winter was over and the green
knobs appeared and began to rise, and to cre-
ate their many hearts. One would say she was
a simple woman, made happy by simple
things. I think this was true. And more than
once, in my long life, I have wished to be her.

Touch-me-nots

The touch-me-nots
were still blooming,
though many had already gone to seed—
jewel of weeds, orange, beloved

of the hummingbirds
for their deeply held sweets,
and the ripe pod, when touched,
so quick

to open and high-fly
its seeds into the world.
I was walking
down a path

where they grew, succulent and thick
in the damp earth near
a stream, when I saw
a trap

with a little raccoon inside,
praying,
as it felt, over and over,
the mesh of its capture,

and I had time—
just time—
to stumble down to the stream, and open the trap,
and say to the little one:

Run, run,
and the little one flew—
I did not touch him—
and climbed high into a tree.

And then I too, knowing the world,
ran through the jewel weeds
as someone, unknown and not smiling,
came down the path to where

the trap lay, stamped upon
by my very own feet,
and while I ran, the touch-me-nots
nodded affirmatively

their golden bodies—
I could not help but touch them—
and dashed forth their sleek pods,
oh, life flew around us, everywhere.

Just Lying on the Grass at Blackwater

I think sometimes of the possible glamour of death—
that it might be wonderful to be
lost and happy inside the green grass—
or to be the green grass!—
or, maybe the pink rose, or the blue iris,
or the affable daisy, or the twirled vine
looping its way skyward—that it might be perfectly peaceful
to be the shining lake, or the hurrying, athletic river,
or the dark shoulders of the trees
where the thrush each evening weeps himself into an ecstasy.

I lie down in the fields of goldenrod, and everlasting.
Who could find me?
My thoughts simplify. I have not done a thousand things
or a hundred things but, perhaps, a few.
As for wondering about answers that are not available except
in books, though in my childhood I was sent there
to find them, I have learned
to leave all that behind

as in summer I take off my shoes and my socks,
my jacket, my hat, and go on
happier, through the fields. The little sparrow
with the pink beak
calls out, over and over, so simply—not to me
but to the whole world. All afternoon
I grow wiser, listening to him,   ⟨

soft, small, nameless fellow at the top of some weed,
enjoying his life. If you can sing, do it. If not,

even silence can feel, to the world, like happiness,
like praise,
from the pool of shade you have found beside the everlasting.

How Would You Live Then?

What if a hundred rose-breasted grosbeaks
    flew in circles around your head? What if
the mockingbird came into the house with you and
    became your advisor? What if
the bees filled your walls with honey and all
    you needed to do was ask them and they would fill
the bowl? What if the brook slid downhill just
    past your bedroom window so you could listen
to its slow prayers as you fell asleep? What if
    the stars began to shout their names, or to run
this way and that way above the clouds? What if
    you painted a picture of a tree, and the leaves
began to rustle, and a bird cheerfully sang
    from its painted branches? What if you suddenly saw
that the silver of water was brighter than the silver
    of money? What if you finally saw
that the sunflowers, turning toward the sun all day
    and every day—who knows how, but they do it—were
more precious, more meaningful than gold?

Old Goldenrod at Field's Edge

Ice upon old
   goldenrod
      stops me at the edge
         of the field, how

gleaming,
   this morning,
      the stiff stalks
         stand,

slender, exhausted,
   the gray boss—
      all that is left of their
         golden hair—

holding
   a crown of snow, and the rest—
      stem and leaves—
         just waiting

in their glass suits
   to fall—
      or, if enduring,
         to see

the great melt, and the fields
   tinged green—
      and the lambs,
         coming again from the

cozy barn,
   with their crazy prancing—
      how the cold
         makes us dream!

FROM

Why I Wake Early

———— ❦ ————

(2 0 0 4)

Why I Wake Early

Hello, sun in my face.
Hello, you who make the morning
and spread it over the fields
and into the faces of the tulips
and the nodding morning glories,
and into the windows of, even, the
miserable and the crotchety—

best preacher that ever was,
dear star, that just happens
to be where you are in the universe
to keep us from ever-darkness,
to ease us with warm touching,
to hold us in the great hands of light—
good morning, good morning, good morning.

Watch, now, how I start the day
in happiness, in kindness.

Bone

Understand, I am always trying to figure out
what the soul is,
and where hidden,
and what shape—

and so, last week,
when I found on the beach
the ear bone
of a pilot whale that may have died

hundreds of years ago, I thought
maybe I was close
to discovering something—
for the ear bone

2.

is the portion that lasts longest
in any of us, man or whale; shaped
like a squat spoon
with a pink scoop where

once, in the lively swimmer's head,
it joined its two sisters
in the house of hearing,
it was only

two inches long—
and I thought: the soul
might be like this—
so hard, so necessary—

3.

yet almost nothing.
Beside me
the gray sea
was opening and shutting its wave-doors,

unfolding over and over
its time-ridiculing roar;
I looked but I couldn't see anything
through its dark-knit glare;

yet don't we all *know,* the golden sand
is there at the bottom,
though our eyes have never seen it,
nor can our hands ever catch it

4.

lest we would sift it down
into fractions, and facts—
certainties—
and what the soul is, also

I believe I will never quite know.
Though I play at the edges of knowing,
truly I know
our part is not knowing,

but looking, and touching, and loving,
which is the way I walked on,
softly,
through the pale-pink morning light.

Freshen the Flowers, She Said

So I put them in the sink, for the cool porcelain
    was tender,
and took out the tattered and cut each stem
    on a slant,
trimmed the black and raggy leaves, and set them all—
    roses, delphiniums, daisies, iris, lilies,
and more whose names I don't know, in bright new water—
    gave them

a bounce upward at the end to let them take
    their own choice of position, the wheels, the spurs,
the little sheds of the buds. It took, to do this,
    perhaps fifteen minutes.
Fifteen minutes of music
    with nothing playing.

Beans

They're not like peaches or squash.
Plumpness isn't for them. They like
being lean, as if for the narrow
path. The beans themselves sit qui-
etly inside their green pods. In-
stinctively one picks with care,
never tearing down the fine vine,
never not noticing their crisp bod-
ies, or feeling their willingness for
the pot, for the fire.

I have thought sometimes that
something—I can't name it—
watches as I walk the rows, accept-
ing the gift of their lives to assist
mine.

I know what you think: this is fool-
ishness. They're only vegetables.
Even the blossoms with which they
begin are small and pale, hardly sig-
nificant. Our hands, or minds, our
feet hold more intelligence. With
this I have no quarrel.

But, what about virtue?

The Poet Goes to Indiana

I'll tell you a half-dozen things
that happened to me
in Indiana
when I went that far west to teach.
You tell me if it was worth it.

I lived in the country
with my dog—
part of the bargain of coming.
And there was a pond
with fish from, I think, China.
I felt them sometimes against my feet.
Also, they crept out of the pond, along its edges,
to eat the grass.
I'm not lying.
And I saw coyotes,
two of them, at dawn, running over the seemingly
unenclosed fields.
And once a deer, but a buck, thick-necked, leaped
into the road just—oh, I mean just, in front of my car—
and we both made it home safe.
And once the blacksmith came to care for the four horses,
or the three horses that belonged to the owner of the house,
and I bargained with him, if I could catch the fourth,
he, too, would have hooves trimmed
for the Indiana winter,
and apples did it,
and a rope over the neck did it,

so I won something wonderful;
and there was, one morning,
an owl
flying, oh pale angel, into
the hayloft of a barn,
I see it still;
and there was once, oh wonderful,
a new horse in the pasture,
a tall, slim being—a neighbor was keeping her there—
and she put her face against my face,
put her muzzle, her nostrils, soft as violets,
against my mouth and my nose, and breathed me,
to see who I was,
a long quiet minute—minutes—
then she stamped feet and whisked tail
and danced deliciously into the grass away, and came back.
She was saying, so plainly, that I was good, or good enough.
Such a fine time I had teaching in Indiana.

The Snow Cricket

Just beyond the leaves and the white faces
of the lilies,
I saw the wings
of the green snow cricket

as it went flying
from vine to vine,
searching, then finding a shadowed place in which
to sit and sing—

and by singing I mean, in this instance,
not just the work of the little mouth-cave,
but of every enfoldment of the body—
a singing that has no words

or a single bar of music
or anything more, in fact, than one repeated
rippling phrase
built of loneliness

and its consequences: longing
and hope.
Pale and humped,
the snow cricket sat all evening

in a leafy hut, in the honeysuckle.
It was trembling
with the force
of its crying out,

and in truth I couldn't wait to see if another would come to it
        .   for fear that it wouldn't,
and I wouldn't be able to bear it.
I wished it good luck, with all my heart,

and went back over the lawn, to where the lilies were standing
on their calm, cob feet,
each in the ease
of a single, waxy body

breathing contentedly in the chill night air;
and I swear I pitied them, as I looked down
into the theater of their perfect faces—
that frozen, bottomless glare.

This World

I would like to write a poem about the world that has in it
nothing fancy.
But it seems impossible.
Whatever the subject, the morning sun
glimmers it.
The tulip feels the heat and flaps its petals open
and becomes a star.
The ants bore into the peony bud and there is the dark
   pinprick well of sweetness.
As for the stones on the beach, forget it.
Each one could be set in gold.
So I tried with my eyes shut, but of course the birds
   were singing.
And the aspen trees were shaking the sweetest music
   out of their leaves.
And that was followed by, guess what, a momentous and
   beautiful silence
as comes to all of us, in little earfuls, if we're not too
   hurried to hear it.
As for spiders, how the dew hangs in their webs
   even if they say nothing, or seem to say nothing.
So fancy is the world, who knows, maybe they sing.
So fancy is the world, who knows, maybe the stars sing too,
   and the ants, and the peonies, and the warm stones,
so happy to be where they are, on the beach, instead of being
   locked up in gold.

Snow Geese

Oh, to love what is lovely, and will not last!
    What a task
      to ask

of anything, or anyone,

yet it is ours,
   and not by the century or the year, but by the hours.

One fall day I heard
  above me, and above the sting of the wind, a sound
I did not know, and my look shot upward; it was

a flock of snow geese, winging it
   faster than the ones we usually see,
and, being the color of snow, catching the sun

so they were, in part at least, golden. I

held my breath
as we do
sometimes
to stop time
when something wonderful
has touched us

as with a match
which is lit, and bright,
but does not hurt
in the common way,

but delightfully,
as if delight
were the most serious thing
you ever felt.

The geese
flew on.
I have never
seen them again.

Maybe I will, someday, somewhere.
Maybe I won't.
It doesn't matter.
What matters
is that, when I saw them,
I saw them
as through the veil, secretly, joyfully, clearly.

Bear

It's not my track,
I say, seeing
the ball of the foot and the wide heel
and the naily, untrimmed
toes. And I say again,
for emphasis,

to no one but myself, since no one is
with me. This is
not my track, and this is an extremely
large foot, I wonder
how large a body must be to make
such a track, I am beginning to make

bad jokes. I have read probably
a hundred narratives where someone saw
just what I am seeing. Various things
happened next. A fairly long list, I won't

go into it. But not one of them told
what happened next—I mean, before whatever happens—

how the distances light up, how the clouds
are the most lovely shapes you have ever seen, how

the wild flowers at your feet begin distilling a fragrance
different, and sweeter than any you ever stood upon before—how

every leaf on the whole mountain is aflutter.

Many Miles

The feet of the heron,
under those bamboo stems,
hold the blue body,
the great beak

above the shallows
of the pond.
Who could guess
their patience?

Sometimes the toes
shake, like worms.
What fish
could resist?

Or think of the cricket,
his green hooks
climbing the blade of grass—
or think of camel feet

like ear muffs,
striding over the sand—
or think of your own
slapping along the highway,

a long life,
many miles.
To each of us comes
the body gift.

The Old Poets of China

Wherever I am, the world comes after me.
It offers me its busyness. It does not believe
that I do not want it. Now I understand
why the old poets of China went so far and high
into the mountains, then crept into the pale mist.

White-eyes

In winter
   all the singing is in
      the tops of the trees
         where the wind-bird

with its white eyes
   shoves and pushes
      among the branches.
         Like any of us

he wants to go to sleep,
   but he's restless—
      he has an idea,
         and slowly it unfolds

from under his beating wings
   as long as he stays awake.
      But his big, round music, after all,
         is too breathy to last.

So, it's over.
   In the pine-crown
      he makes his nest,
         he's done all he can.

I don't know the name of this bird,
   I only imagine his glittering beak
      tucked in a white wing
         while the clouds—

which he has summoned
    from the north—
        which he has taught
            to be mild, and silent—

thicken, and begin to fall
    into the world below
        like stars, or the feathers
            of some unimaginable bird

that loves us,
    that is asleep now, and silent—
        that has turned itself
            into snow.

Some Things, Say the Wise Ones

Some things, say the wise ones who know everything,
are not living. I say,
you live your life your way and leave me alone.

I have talked with the faint clouds in the sky when they
are afraid of being left behind; I have said, Hurry, hurry!
and they have said: thank you, we are hurrying.

About cows, and starfish, and roses, there is no
argument. They die, after all.

But water is a question, so many living things in it,
but what is it, itself, living or not? Oh, gleaming

generosity, how can they write you out?

As I think this I am sitting on the sand beside
the harbor. I am holding in my hand
small pieces of granite, pyrite, schist.
Each one, just now, so thoroughly asleep.

Mindful

Every day
   I see or I hear
     something
       that more or less

kills me
   with delight,
     that leaves me
       like a needle

in the haystack
   of light.
     It is what I was born for—
       to look, to listen,

to lose myself
   inside this soft world—
     to instruct myself
       over and over

in joy,
   and acclamation.
     Nor am I talking
       about the exceptional,

the fearful, the dreadful,
   the very extravagant—
     but of the ordinary,
       the common, the very drab,

the daily presentations.
   Oh, good scholar,
      I say to myself,
         how can you help

but grow wise
   with such teachings
      as these—
         the untrimmable light

of the world,
   the ocean's shine,
      the prayers that are made
      out of grass?

Song of the Builders

On a summer morning
I sat down
on a hillside
to think about God—

a worthy pastime.
Near me, I saw
a single cricket;
it was moving the grains of the hillside

this way and that way.
How great was its energy,
how humble its effort.
Let us hope

it will always be like this,
each of us going on
in our inexplicable ways
building the universe.

Daisies

It is possible, I suppose, that sometime
   we will learn everything
there is to learn: what the world is, for example,
   and what it means. I think this as I am crossing
from one field to another, in summer, and the
   mockingbird is mocking me, as one who either
knows enough already or knows enough to be
   perfectly content not knowing. Song being born
of quest he knows this: he must turn silent
   were he suddenly assaulted with answers. Instead

oh hear his wild, caustic, tender warbling ceaselessly
   unanswered. At my feet the white-petaled daisies display
the small suns of their center-piece, their—if you don't
   mind my saying so—their hearts. Of course
I could be wrong, perhaps their hearts are pale and
   narrow and hidden in the roots. What do I know.
But this: it is heaven itself to take what is given,
   to see what is plain; what the sun
lights up willingly; for example—I think this
   as I reach down, not to pick but merely to touch—
the suitability of the field for the daisies, and the
   daisies for the field.

The Soul at Last

The Lord's terrifying kindness has come to me.

It was only a small silvery thing—say a piece of silver cloth, or a thousand spider webs woven together, or a small handful of aspen leaves, with their silver backs shimmering. And it came leaping out of the closed coffin; it flew into the air, it danced snappingly around the church rafters, it vanished through the ceiling.

I spoke there, briefly, of the loved one gone. I gazed at the people in the pews, some of them weeping. I knew I must, someday, write this down.

Lingering in Happiness

After rain after many days without rain,
it stays cool, private and cleansed, under the trees,
and the dampness there, married now to gravity,
falls branch to branch, leaf to leaf, down to the ground

where it will disappear—but not, of course, vanish
except to our eyes. The roots of the oaks will have their share,
and the white threads of the grasses, and the cushion of moss;
a few drops, round as pearls, will enter the mole's tunnel;

and soon so many small stones, buried for a thousand years,
will feel themselves being touched.

FROM

Owls and Other Fantasies

———— ❧ ————

(2 0 0 3)

The Dipper

Once I saw
in a quick-falling, white-veined stream,
among the leafed islands of the wet rocks,
a small bird, and knew it

from the pages of a book; it was
the dipper, and dipping he was,
as well as, sometimes, on a rock-peak, starting up
the clear, strong pipe of his voice; at this,

there being no words to transcribe, I had to
bend forward, as it were,
into his frame of mind, catching
everything I could in the tone,

cadence, sweetness, and briskness
of his affirmative report.
Though not by words, it was
a more than satisfactory way to the

bridge of understanding. This happened
in Colorado
more than half a century ago—
more, certainly, than half my lifetime ago—

and, just as certainly, he has been sleeping for decades
in the leaves beside the stream,
his crumble of white bones, his curl of flesh
comfortable even so.

And still I hear him—
and whenever I open the ponderous book of riddles
he sits with his black feet hooked to the page,
his eyes cheerful, still burning with water-love—

and thus the world is full of leaves and feathers,
and comfort, and instruction. I do not even remember
your name, great river,
but since that hour I have lived

simply,
in the joy of the body as full and clear
as falling water; the pleasures of the mind
like a dark bird dipping in and out, tasting and singing.

Spring

All day the flicker
has anticipated
the lust of the season, by
shouting. He scouts up
tree after tree and at
a certain place begins
to cry out. My, in his
black-freckled vest, bay body with
red trim and sudden chrome
underwings, he is
dapper. Of course somebody
listening nearby
hears him; she answers
with a sound like hysterical
laughter, and rushes out into
the field where he is poised
on an old phone pole, his head
swinging, his wings
opening and shutting in a kind of
butterfly stroke. She can't
resist; they touch; they flutter.
How lightly, altogether, they accept
the great task, of carrying life
forward! In the crown of an oak
they choose a small tree-cave

which they enter with sudden quietness
and modesty. And, for a while,
the wind that can be
a knife or a hammer, subsides.
They listen
to the thrushes.
The sky is blue, or the rain
falls with its spills of pearl.
Around their wreath of darkness
the leaves of the world unfurl.

Goldfinches

Some goldfinches were having a melodious argument at the edge of a puddle. The birds wanted to bathe, or perhaps just to dip their heads and look at themselves, and they were having trouble with who should be first, and so on. So they discussed it while I stood in the distance, listening. Perhaps in Tibet, in the old holy places, they also have such fragile bells. Or are these birds really just that, bells come to us—come to this road in America—let us bow our heads and remember now how we used to do it, say a prayer. Meanwhile the birds bathe and splash and have a good time. Then they fly off, their dark wings opening from their bright, yellow bodies; their tiny feet, all washed, clasping the air.

Such Singing in the Wild Branches

It was spring
and finally I heard him
among the first leaves—
then I saw him clutching the limb

in an island of shade
with his red-brown feathers
all trim and neat for the new year.
First, I stood still

and thought of nothing.
Then I began to listen.
Then I was filled with gladness—
and that's when it happened,

when I seemed to float,
to be, myself, a wing or a tree—
and I began to understand
what the bird was saying,

and the sands in the glass
stopped
for a pure white moment
while gravity sprinkled upward

like rain, rising,
and in fact

it became difficult to tell just what it was that was singing—
it was the thrush for sure, but it seemed

not a single thrush, but himself, and all his brothers,
and also the trees around them,
as well as the gliding, long-tailed clouds
in the perfectly blue sky—all, all of them

were singing.
And, of course, so it seemed,
so was I.
Such soft and solemn and perfect music doesn't last

for more than a few moments.
It's one of those magical places wise people
like to talk about.
One of the things they say about it, that is true,

is that, once you've been there,
you're there forever.
Listen, everyone has a chance.
Is it spring, is it morning?

Are there trees near you,
and does your own soul need comforting?
Quick, then—open the door and fly on your heavy feet; the song
may already be drifting away.

While I Am Writing a Poem to Celebrate Summer, the Meadowlark Begins to Sing

Sixty-seven years, oh Lord, to look at the clouds,
the trees in deep, moist summer,

daisies and morning glories
opening every morning

their small, ecstatic faces—
Or maybe I should just say

how I wish I had a voice
like the meadowlark's,

sweet, clear, and reliably
slurring all day long

from the fencepost, or the long grass
where it lives

in a tiny but adequate grass hut
beside the mullein and the everlasting,

the faint-pink roses
that have never been improved, but come to bud

then open like little soft sighs
under the meadowlark's whistle, its breath-praise,

its thrill-song, its anthem, its thanks, its
alleluia. Alleluia, oh Lord.

Long Afternoon at the Edge of
Little Sister Pond

As for life,
I'm humbled,
I'm without words
sufficient to say

how it has been hard as flint,
and soft as a spring pond,
both of these
and over and over,

and long pale afternoons besides,
and so many mysteries
beautiful as eggs in a nest,
still unhatched

though warm and watched over
by something I have never seen—
a tree angel, perhaps,
or a ghost of holiness.

Every day I walk out into the world
to be dazzled, then to be reflective.

It suffices, it is all comfort—
along with human love,

dog love, water love, little-serpent love,
sunburst love, or love for that smallest of birds
flying among the scarlet flowers.
There is hardly time to think about

stopping, and lying down at last
to the long afterlife, to the tenderness
yet to come, when
time will brim over the singular pond, and become forever,

and we will pretend to melt away into the leaves.
As for death,
I can't wait to be the hummingbird,
can you?

FROM

Winter Hours

—— ❧ ——

(1 9 9 9)

Three Prose Poems

1

Oh, yesterday, that one, we all cry out. *Oh, that one!* How rich and possible everything was! How ripe, ready, lavish, and filled with excitement—how hopeful we were on those summer days, under the clean, white racing clouds. *Oh, yesterday!*

2

I was in the old burn-dump—no longer used—where the honeysuckle all summer is in a moist rage, willing it would seem to be enough to decorate the whole world. Here a pair of hummingbirds lived every summer, as if the only ones of their kind, in their own paradise at the side of the high road. On hot afternoons, beside the blackberry canes that rose thickly from that wrecked place, I strolled, and was almost always sure to see the male hummingbird on his favorite high perch, near the top of a wild cherry tree, looking out across his kingdom with bright eye and even brighter throat. And then, on the afternoon I am telling about, as he swung his head, there came out of the heavens an immense growl, of metal and energy, shoving and shrilling, boring through the air. And a plane, a black triangle, flew screaming from the horizon, heavy talons clenched and lumpy on its underside. Immediately: a suffering in the head, through the narrow-channeled ears. And I saw the small bird, in the sparkle of its tree, fling its green head sideways for the eye to see this hawk-bird, this nightmare pressing overhead. And, lo, the hummingbird cringed, it hugged itself to the limb, it hunkered, it quivered. It was God's gorgeous, flashing jewel: afraid.

All narrative is metaphor.

3

After the storm the ocean returned without fanfare to its old offices; the tide climbed onto the snow-covered shore and then receded; so there was the world: sky, water, the pale sand and, where the tide had reached that day's destination, the snow.

And this detail: the body of a duck, a golden-eye; and beside it one black-backed gull. In the body of the duck, among the breast feathers, a hole perhaps an inch across; the color within the hole a shouting red. And bend it as you might, nothing was to blame: storms must toss, and the great black-backed gawker must eat, and so on. It was merely a moment. The sun, angling out from the bunched clouds, cast one could easily imagine tenderly over the landscape its extraordinary light.

Moss

Maybe the idea of the world as flat isn't a tribal memory or an archetypal memory, but something far older—a fox memory, a worm memory, a moss memory.

Memory of leaping or crawling or shrugging rootlet by rootlet forward, across the flatness of everything.

To perceive of the earth as round needed something else —standing up!—that hadn't yet happened.

What a wild family! Fox and giraffe and wart hog, of course. But these also: bodies like tiny strings, bodies like blades and blossoms! Cord grass, Christmas fern, soldier moss! And here comes grasshopper, all toes and knees and eyes, over the little mountains of dust.

When I see the black cricket in the woodpile, in autumn, I don't frighten her. And when I see the moss grazing upon the rock, I touch her tenderly,

sweet cousin.

The Whistler

All of a sudden she began to whistle. By all of a sudden
I mean that for more than thirty years she had not
whistled. It was thrilling. At first I wondered, who was
in the house, what stranger? I was upstairs reading, and
she was downstairs. As from the throat of a wild and
cheerful bird, not caught but visiting, the sounds war-
bled and slid and doubled back and larked and soared.

Finally I said, Is that you? Is that you whistling? Yes, she
said. I used to whistle, a long time ago. Now I see I can
still whistle. And cadence after cadence she strolled
through the house, whistling.

I know her so well, I think. I thought. Elbow and an-
kle. Mood and desire. Anguish and frolic. Anger too.
And the devotions. And for all that, do we even begin
to know each other? Who is this I've been living with
for thirty years?

This clear, dark, lovely whistler?

The Storm

Now through the white orchard my little dog
    romps, breaking the new snow
    with wild feet.
Running here running there, excited,
    hardly able to stop, he leaps, he spins
until the white snow is written upon
    in large, exuberant letters,
a long sentence, expressing
    the pleasures of the body in this world.

Oh, I could not have said it better
    myself.

FROM

West Wind

❦

(1 9 9 7)

Seven White Butterflies

Seven white butterflies
delicate in a hurry look
how they bang the pages
 of their wings as they fly

to the fields of mustard yellow
and orange and plain
gold all eternity
 is in the moment this is what

Blake said Whitman said such
wisdom in the agitated
motions of the mind seven
 dancers floating

even as worms toward
paradise see how they banter
and riot and rise
 to the trees flutter

lob their white bodies into
the invisible wind weightless
lacy willing
 to deliver themselves unto

the universe now each settles
down on a yellow thumb on a
brassy stem now
 all seven are rapidly sipping

from the golden towers who
would have thought it could be so easy?

At Round Pond

owl
make your little appearance now

owl dark bird bird of gloom
messenger reminder

of death
that can't be stopped

argued with leashed put out
like a red fire but

burns as it will
owl

I have not seen you now for
too long a time don't

hide away but come flowing and clacking
the slap of your wings

your death's head oh rise
out of the thick and shaggy pines when you

look down with your
golden eyes how everything

trembles
then settles

from mere incidence into
the lush of meaning.

The Dog Has Run Off Again

and I should start shouting his name
and clapping my hands,
but it has been raining all night
and the narrow creek has risen
is a tawny turbulence is rushing along
over the mossy stones
is surging forward
with a sweet loopy music
and therefore I don't want to entangle it
with my own voice
calling summoning
my little dog to hurry back
look the sunlight and the shadows are chasing each other
listen how the wind swirls and leaps and dives up and down
who am I to summon his hard and happy body
his four white feet that love to wheel and pedal
through the dark leaves
to come back to walk by my side, obedient.

Am I Not Among the Early Risers

Am I not among the early risers
and the long-distance walkers?

Have I not stood, amazed, as I consider
the perfection of the morning star
above the peaks of the houses, and the crowns of the trees
    blue in the first light?
Do I not see how the trees tremble, as though
    sheets of water flowed over them
though it is only wind, that common thing,
    free to everyone, and everything?

Have I not thought, for years, what it would be
worthy to do, and then gone off, barefoot and with a silver pail,
    to gather blueberries,
thus coming, as I think, upon a right answer?

What will ambition do for me that the fox, appearing suddenly
at the top of the field,
her eyes sharp and confident as she stared into mine,
has not already done?

What countries, what visitations,
    what pomp
would satisfy me as thoroughly as Blackwater Woods
on a sun-filled morning, or, equally, in the rain?

Here is an amazement—once I was twenty years old and in
    every motion of my body there was a delicious ease,
and in every motion of the green earth there was
    a hint of paradise,
and now I am sixty years old, and it is the same.

Above the modest house and the palace—the same darkness.
Above the evil man and the just, the same stars.
Above the child who will recover and the child who will
     not recover, the same energies roll forward,
from one tragedy to the next and from one foolishness to the next.

     I bow down.

Have I not loved as though the beloved could vanish at any moment,
or become preoccupied, or whisper a name other than mine
     in the stretched curvatures of lust, or over the dinner table?
Have I ever taken good fortune for granted?

Have I not, every spring, befriended the swarm that pours forth?
Have I not summoned the honey-man to come, to hurry,
     to bring with him the white and comfortable hive?

And, while I waited, have I not leaned close, to see everything?
Have I not been stung as I watched their milling and gleaming,
     and stung hard?

Have I not been ready always at the iron door,
     not knowing to what country it opens—to death or to more life?

Have I ever said that the day was too hot or too cold
or the night too long and as black as oil anyway,
or the morning, washed blue and emptied entirely
     of the second-rate, less than happiness

as I stepped down from the porch and set out along
the green paths of the world?

Stars

Here in my head, language
keeps making its tiny noises.

How can I hope to be friends
with the hard white stars

whose flaring and hissing are not speech
but a pure radiance?

How can I hope to be friends
with the yawning spaces between them

where nothing, ever, is spoken?
Tonight, at the edge of the field,

I stood very still, and looked up,
and tried to be empty of words.

What joy was it, that almost found me?
What amiable peace?

Then it was over, the wind
roused up in the oak trees behind me

and I fell back, easily.
Earth has a hundred thousand pure contraltos—

even the distant night bird
as it talks threat, as it talks love

over the cold, black fields.
Once, deep in the woods,

I found the white skull of a bear
and it was utterly silent—

and once a river otter, in a steel trap,
and it too was utterly silent.

What can we do
but keep on breathing in and out,

modest and willing, and in our places?
Listen, listen, I'm forever saying.

Listen to the river, to the hawk, to the hoof,
to the mockingbird, to the jack-in-the-pulpit—

then I come up with a few words, like a gift.
Even as now.

Even as the darkness has remains the pure, deep darkness.
Even as the stars have twirled a little, while I stood here,

looking up,
one hot sentence after another.

Forty Years

for forty years
the sheets of white paper have
passed under my hands and I have tried
    to improve their peaceful

emptiness putting down
little curls little shafts
of letters words
    little flames leaping

not one page
was less to me than fascinating
discursive full of cadence
    its pale nerves hiding

in the curves of the Qs
behind the soldierly Hs
in the webbed feet of the Ws
    forty years

and again this morning as always
I am stopped as the world comes back
wet and beautiful I am thinking
    that language

is not even a river
is not a tree is not a green field

is not even a black ant traveling
    briskly modestly

from day to day from one
golden page to another.

Little Summer Poem Touching the Subject of Faith

Every summer
   I listen and look
      under the sun's brass and even
         in the moonlight, but I can't hear

anything, I can't see anything—
   not the pale roots digging down, nor the green stalks muscling up,
      nor the leaves
         deepening their damp pleats,

nor the tassels making,
   nor the shucks, nor the cobs.
      And still,
         every day,

the leafy fields
   grow taller and thicker—
      green gowns lofting up in the night,
         showered with silk.

And so, every summer,
   I fail as a witness, seeing nothing—
      I am deaf too
         to the tick of the leaves,

the tapping of downwardness from the banyan feet—
   all of it
      happening
         beyond all seeable proof, or hearable hum.

And, therefore, let the immeasurable come.
    Let the unknowable touch the buckle of my spine.
        Let the wind turn in the trees,
            and the mystery hidden in dirt

swing through the air.
    How could I look at anything in this world
        and tremble, and grip my hands over my heart?
        What should I fear?

One morning
    in the leafy green ocean
        the honeycomb of the corn's beautiful body
          is sure to be there.

Dogs

Over
the wide field

the dark deer
went running,

five dogs
screaming

at his flanks,
at his heels,

my own two darlings
among them

lunging and buckling
with desire

as they leaped
for the throat

as they tried
and tried again

to bring him down.
At the lake

the deer
plunged—

I could hear
the green wind

of his breath
tearing

but the long legs
never stopped

till he clambered
up the far shore.

The dogs
moaned and screeched

they flung themselves
on the grass

panting
and steaming.

It took hours
but finally

in the half-drowned light
in the silence

of the summer evening
they woke

from fitful naps,
they stepped

in their old good natures
toward us

look look
into their eyes

bright as planets
under the long lashes

here is such happiness when you speak their names!
here is such unforced love!

here is such shyness such courage!
here is the shining rudimentary soul

here is hope retching, the world as it is
here is the black the red the bottomless pool.

West Wind

1

If there is life after the earth-life, will you come with me?
Even then? Since we're bound to be something, why not
together. Imagine! Two little stones, two fleas under the
wing of a gull, flying along through the fog! Or, ten blades
of grass. Ten loops of honeysuckle, all flung against each
other, at the edge of Race Road! Beach plums! Snowflakes,
coasting into the winter woods, making a very small sound,
like this

soooooooooooooooooooooooooooooooooooooooooooo

as they marry the dusty bodies of the pitch-pines. Or, rain—
that gray light running over the sea, pocking it, lacquering
it, coming, all morning and afternoon, from the west wind's
youth and abundance and jollity—pinging and jangling
down upon the roofs of Provincetown.

2

You are young. So you know everything. You leap
into the boat and begin rowing. But, listen to me.
Without fanfare, without embarrassment, without
any doubt, I talk directly to your soul. Listen to me.
Lift the oars from the water, let your arms rest, and
your heart, and heart's little intelligence, and listen to
me. There is life without love. It is not worth a bent
penny, or a scuffed shoe. It is not worth the body of a
dead dog nine days unburied. When you hear, a mile
away and still out of sight, the churn of the water
as it begins to swirl and roil, fretting around the
sharp rocks—when you hear that unmistakable
pounding—when you feel the mist on your mouth
and sense ahead the embattlement, the long falls
plunging and steaming—then row, row for your life
toward it.

3

And the speck of my heart, in my shed of flesh
and bone, began to sing out, the way the sun
would sing if the sun could sing, if light had a
mouth and a tongue, if the sky had a throat, if
god wasn't just an idea but shoulders and a spine,
gathered from everywhere, even the most distant
planets, blazing up. Where am I? Even the rough
words come to me now, quick as thistles. Who
made your tyrant's body, your thirst, your delv-
ing, your gladness? Oh tiger, oh bone-breaker,
oh tree on fire! Get away from me. Come closer.

7

We see Bill only occasionally, when we stop by the antique shop that's on the main hot highway to Charlottesville. Usually he's alone—his wife is dead—but sometimes his son will be with him, or idling just outside in the yard. Once M. bought a small glass ship from the boy, it had chips of colored glass for sails and cost two dollars, the boy was greatly pleased.

Today Bill tells us—for a mockingbird has begun to sing—how a friend came during the summer and filled a bowl with fruit from the cherry tree. Then, leaving the bowl on the stoop, he went inside to sit with Bill at the kitchen table. Together Bill and his friend watched the mockingbird come to the bowl, take the cherries one by one, fly back across the yard and drop them under the branches of the tree. When the bowl was empty the bird settled again in the leaves and began to sing vigorously.

At the back of the shop and here and there on the dusty shelves are piled the useless broken things one couldn't ever sell—bits of rusty metal, and odd pieces of china, a cup or a plate with a fraction of its design still clear: a garden, or a span of country bridge leading from one happiness or another, or part of a house. Once Bill told us, almost shyly, how much the boy is coming to resemble his mother. Through the open window we can hear the mockingbird, still young, still lucky, wild beak kissing and chuckling as it flutters and struts along the avenue of song.

8

The young, tall English poet—soon to die, soon to sail on his small boat into the blue haze and then the storm and then under the gray waves' spinning threshold—went over to Pisa to meet a friend; met him; spent with him a sunny afternoon. I love this poet, which means nothing here or there, but is like a garden in my heart. So my love is a gift to myself. And I think of him, on that July afternoon in Pisa, while his friend Hunt told him stories pithy and humorous, of their friends in England, so that he began to laugh, so that his tall, lean body shook, and his long legs couldn't hold him, and he had to lean up against the building, seized with laughter, abundant and unstoppable; and so he leaned in the wild sun, against the stones of the building, with the tears flying from his eyes—full of foolishness, howling, hanging on to the stones, crawling with laughter, clasping his own body as it began to fly apart in the nonsense, the sweetness, the intelligence, the bright happiness falling, like tiny gold flowers, like the sunlight itself, the lilt of Hunt's voice, on this simple afternoon, with a friend, in Pisa.

9

And what did you think love would be like?
A summer day? The brambles in their places,
and the long stretches of mud? Flowers in every
field, in every garden, with their soft beaks and
their pastel shoulders? On one street after an-
other, the litter ticks in the gutter. In one room
after another, the lovers meet, quarrel, sicken,
break apart, cry out. One or two leap from
windows. Most simply lean, exhausted, their
thin arms on the sill. They have done all that
they could. The golden eagle, that lives not far
from here, has perhaps a thousand tiny feathers
flowing from the back of its head, each one
shaped like an infinitely small but perfect spear.

Have You Ever Tried to Enter the Long Black Branches

Have you ever tried to enter the long black branches
    of other lives—
tried to imagine what the crisp fringes, full of honey,
    hanging
from the branches of the young locust trees, in early summer,
    feel like?

Do you think this world is only an entertainment for you?

Never to enter the sea and notice how the water divides
    with perfect courtesy, to let you in!
Never to lie down on the grass, as though you were the grass!
Never to leap to the air as you open your wings over
    the dark acorn of your heart!

No wonder we hear, in your mournful voice, the complaint
    that something is missing from your life!

Who can open the door who does not reach for the latch?
Who can travel the miles who does not put one foot
    in front of the other, all attentive to what presents itself
    continually?
Who will behold the inner chamber who has not observed
    with admiration, even with rapture, the outer stone?

Well, there is time left—
fields everywhere invite you into them.

And who will care, who will chide you if you wander away
    from wherever you are, to look for your soul?

Quickly, then, get up, put on your coat, leave your desk!

To put one's foot into the door of the grass, which is
    the mystery, which is death as well as life, and
    not be afraid!

To set one's foot in the door of death, and be overcome
    with amazement!

To sit down in front of the weeds, and imagine
    god the ten-fingered, sailing out of his house of straw,

nodding this way and that way, to the flowers of the
    present hour,

to the song falling out of the mockingbird's pink mouth,

to the tiplets of the honeysuckle, that have opened
    in the night.

To sit down, like a weed among weeds, and rustle in the wind!

Listen, are you breathing just a little, and calling it a life?

While the soul, after all, is only a window,
and the opening of the window no more difficult
than the wakening from a little sleep.

Only last week I went out among the thorns and said
    to the wild roses:
deny me not,
but suffer my devotion.
Then, all afternoon, I sat among them. Maybe

I even heard a curl or two of music, damp and rouge-red,
hurrying from their stubby buds, from their delicate watery bodies.

For how long will you continue to listen to those dark shouters,
    caution and prudence?

Fall in! Fall in!

A woman standing in the weeds.
A small boat flounders in the deep waves, and what's coming next
    is coming with its own heave and grace.

Meanwhile, once in a while, I have chanced, among the quick things,
    upon the immutable.
What more could one ask?

And I would touch the faces of the daisies,
and I would bow down
to think about it.

That was then, which hasn't ended yet.

Now the sun begins to swing down. Under the peach-light,
I cross the fields and the dunes, I follow the ocean's edge.

I climb. I backtrack.
I float.
I ramble my way home.

FROM

White Pine

———— ❦ ————

(1 9 9 4)

Work

How beautiful
this morning
was Pasture Pond.

It had lain in the dark, all night,
catching the rain

on its broad back.
All day I work
with the linen of words

and the pins of punctuation
all day I hang out
over a desk

grinding my teeth
staring.
Then I sleep.

Then I come out of the house,
even before the sun is up,

and walk back through the pinewoods
to Pasture Pond.

May

What lay on the road was no mere handful of snake. It was the copperhead at last, golden under the street lamp. I hope to see everything in this world before I die. I knelt on the road and stared. Its head was wedge-shaped and fell back to the unexpected slimness of a neck. The body itself was thick, tense, electric. Clearly this wasn't black snake looking down from the limbs of a tree, or green snake, or the garter, whizzing over the rocks. Where these had, oh, such shyness, this one had none. When I moved a little, it turned and clamped its eyes on mine; then it jerked toward me. I jumped back and watched as it flowed on across the road and down into the dark. My heart was pounding. I stood a while, listening to the small sounds of the woods and looking at the stars. After excitement we are so restful. When the thumb of fear lifts, we are so alive.

Beside the Waterfall

At dawn
   the big dog—
      Winston by name—
         reached down

into the leaves—tulips and willows mostly—
   beside the white
      waterfall,
         and dragged out,

into plain sight,
   a fawn;
      it was scarcely larger
         than a rabbit

and, thankfully,
   it was dead.
      Winston
         looked over the

delicate, spotted body and then
   deftly
      tackled
         the beautiful flower-like head,

breaking it and
   breaking it off and
      swallowing it.
         All the while this was happening

it was growing lighter.
    When I called to him
        Winston merely looked up.
           Grizzled around the chin

and with kind eyes,
    he, too, if you're willing,
        had a face
           like a flower; and then the red sun,

which had been rising all the while anyway,
    broke
        clear of the trees and dropped its wild, clawed light
        over everything.

Yes! No!

How necessary it is to have opinions! I think the spotted trout lilies are satisfied, standing a few inches above the earth. I think serenity is not something you just find in the world, like a plum tree, holding up its white petals.

The violets, along the river, are opening their blue faces, like small dark lanterns.

The green mosses, being so many, are as good as brawny.

How important it is to walk along, not in haste but slowly, looking at everything and calling out

Yes! No! The

swan, for all his pomp, his robes of glass and petals, wants only to be allowed to live on the nameless pond. The catbrier is without fault. The water thrushes, down among the sloppy rocks, are going crazy with happiness. Imagination is better than a sharp instrument. To pay attention, this is our endless and proper work.

In Pobiddy, Georgia

Three women
climb from the car
in which they have driven slowly
into the churchyard.
They come toward us, to see
what we are doing.
What we are doing
is reading the strange,
wonderful names
of the dead.
One of the women
speaks to us—
after we speak to her.
She walks with us and shows us,
with downward-thrust finger,
which of the dead
were her people.
She tells us
about two brothers, and an argument,
and a gun—she points
to one of the slabs
on which there is a name,
some scripture, a handful of red
plastic flowers. We ask her
about the other brother.
"Chain gang," she says,
as you or I might say
"Des Moines," or "New Haven." And then,
"Look around all you want."
The younger woman stands back, in the stiff weeds,

like a banked fire.
The third one—
the oldest human being we have ever seen in our lives—
suddenly drops to the dirt
and begins to cry. Clearly
she is blind, and clearly
she can't rise, but they lift her, like a child,
and lead her away, across the graves, as though,
as old as anything could ever be, she was, finally,
perfectly finished, perfectly heartbroken, perfectly wild.

Mockingbirds

This morning
two mockingbirds
in the green field
were spinning and tossing

the white ribbons
of their songs
into the air.
I had nothing

better to do
than listen.
I mean this
seriously.

In Greece,
a long time ago,
an old couple
opened their door

to two strangers
who were,
it soon appeared,
not men at all,

but gods.
It is my favorite story—
how the old couple
had almost nothing to give

but their willingness
to be attentive—
and for this alone
the gods loved them

and blessed them.
When the gods rose
out of their mortal bodies,
like a million particles of water

from a fountain,
the light
swept into all the corners
of the cottage,

and the old couple,
shaken with understanding,
bowed down—
but still they asked for nothing

beyond the difficult life
which they had already.
And the gods smiled as they vanished,
clapping their great wings.

Wherever it was
I was supposed to be
this morning—
whatever it was I said

I would be doing—
I was standing
at the edge of the field—
I was hurrying

through my own soul,
opening its dark doors—
I was leaning out;
I was listening.

Grass

Those who disappointed, betrayed, scarified! Those who would still put their hands upon me! Those who belong to the past!

How many of us have weighted the years with groaning and weeping? How many years have I done it how many nights spent panting hating grieving, oh, merciless, pitiless remembrances!

I walk over the green hillsides, I lie down on the harsh, sun-flavored blades and bundles of grass; the grass cares nothing about me, it doesn't want anything from me, it rises to its own purpose, and sweetly, following the single holy dictum: to be itself, to let the sky be the sky, to let a young girl be a young girl freely—to let a middle-aged woman be, comfortably, a middle-aged woman.

Those bloody sharps and flats—those endless calamities of the personal past. Bah! I disown them from the rest of my life, in which I mean to rest.

Morning Glories

Blue and dark-blue
  rose and deepest rose
    white and pink they

are everywhere in the diligent
  cornfield rising and swaying
    in their reliable

finery in the little
  fling of their bodies their
    gear and tackle

all caught up in the cornstalks.
  The reaper's story is the story
    of endless work of

work careful and heavy but the
  reaper cannot
    separate them out there they

are in the story of his life
  bright random useless
    year after year

taken with the serious tons
  weeds without value humorous
    beautiful weeds.

August

Our neighbor, tall and blonde and vigorous, the mother of many children, is sick. We did not know she was sick, but she has come to the fence, walking like a woman who is balancing a sword inside of her body, and besides that her long hair is gone, it is short and, suddenly, gray. I don't recognize her. It even occurs to me that it might be her mother. But it's her own laughter-edged voice, we have heard it for years over the hedges.

All summer the children, grown now and some of them with children of their own, come to visit. They swim, they go for long walks along the harbor, they make dinners for twelve, for fifteen, for twenty. In the early morning two daughters come to the garden and slowly go through the precise and silent gestures of T'ai Chi.

They all smile. Their father smiles too, and builds castles on the shore with the children, and drives back to the city, and drives back to the country. A carpenter is hired—a roof re-paired, a porch rebuilt. Everything that can be fixed.

June, July, August. Every day, we hear their laughter. I think of the painting by van Gogh, the man in the chair. Everything wrong, and nowhere to go. His hands over his eyes.

Owl in the Black Oaks

If a lynx, that plush fellow,
climbed down a
tree and left behind
his face, his thick neck,

and, most of all, the lamps of his eyes,
there you would have it—
the owl,
the very owl

who haunts these trees,
choosing from the swash of branches
the slight perches and ledges
of his acrobatics.

Almost every day
I spy him out
among the knots and the burls,
looking down

at his huge feet,
at the path curving through the trees,
at whatever is coming up the hill
toward him,

and, though I'm never ready—
though something unspeakably cold
always drops through my heart—
it is a moment

as lavish as it is fearful—
there is such pomp
in the gown of feathers
and the lit silk of the eyes—

surely he is one of the mighty kings
of this world.
Sometimes, as I keep coming,
he simply flies away—

and sometimes the whole body
tilts forward, and the beak opens,
clean and wonderful,
like a cup of gold.

The Gesture

On the dog's ear, a scrap of filmy stuff
    turns out to be
a walking stick, that jade insect, this one scarcely sprung
    from the pod of the nest,
not an inch long. I could just see
the eyes, elbows, feet nimble under the long shanks.
    I could not imagine it could live
in the brisk world, or where it would live, or how. But
    I took it
outside and held it up to the red oak that rises
    ninety feet into the air, and it lifted its forward-most
        pair of arms
with what in anything worth thinking about would have seemed
    a graceful and glad gesture; it caught
onto the bark, it hung on; it rested; it began to climb.

I Found a Dead Fox

I found a dead fox
beside the gravel road,
curled inside the big
iron wheel

of an old tractor
that has been standing,
for years,
in the vines at the edge

of the road.
I don't know
what happened to it—
when it came there

or why it lay down
for good, settling
its narrow chin
on the rusted rim

of the iron wheel
to look out
over the fields,
and that way died—

but I know
this: its posture—
of looking,
to the last possible moment,

back into the world—
made me want
to sing something
joyous and tender

about foxes.
But what happened is this—
when I began,
when I crawled in

through the honeysuckle
and lay down,
curling my long spine
inside that cold wheel,

and touched the dead fox,
and looked out
into the wide fields,
the fox

vanished.
There was only myself
and the world,
and it was I

who was leaving.
And what could I sing
then?
Oh, beautiful world!

I just lay there
and looked at it.
And then it grew dark.
That day was done with.

And then the stars stepped forth
and held up their appointed fires—
those hot, hard
watchmen of the night.

Toad

I was walking by. He was sitting there.

It was full morning, so the heat was heavy on his sand-colored head and his webbed feet. I squatted beside him, at the edge of the path. He didn't move.

I began to talk. I talked about summer, and about time. The pleasures of eating, the terrors of the night. About this cup we call a life. About happiness. And how good it feels, the heat of the sun between the shoulder blades.

He looked neither up nor down, which didn't necessarily mean he was either afraid or asleep. I felt his energy, stored under his tongue perhaps, and behind his bulging eyes.

I talked about how the world seems to me, five feet tall, the blue sky all around my head. I said, I wondered how it seemed to him, down there, intimate with the dust.

He might have been Buddha—did not move, blink, or frown, not a tear fell from those gold-rimmed eyes as the refined anguish of language passed over him.

Rumor of Moose in the Long Twilight of New Hampshire

Neighbors described

>the high, rough-coated shoulders

the long neck

>the glandular bell hanging

the shy face

>the modest face of a scholar

weary of reading
in the dim light

>of the forest, how he carried

the flared rack

>the knobs the branches

of dense horn

>sign of power

❧

and how he walked

>shaking the flies

rippling his dark pelt

>ponderous on his long bones

into the water

❧

>and how he lifted

frond after frond

>lilies and rushes

onto the path

>of his grinding molars

the light lingered

                  we sat on the shore

and talked in whispers

                  watched the herons

heard the owl

                  greeted the moon

stared at the far shore
stared at the far shore

                  empty in the moonlight

The Sea Mouse

What lay this morning
on the wet sand
was so ugly
I sighed with a kind of horror as I lifted it

into my hand
and looked under the soaked mat of what was almost fur,
but wasn't, and found
the face that has no eyes, and recognized

the sea mouse—
toothless, legless, earless too,
it had been flung out of the stormy sea
and dropped

into the world's outer weather, and clearly it was
done for. I studied
what was not even a fist
of gray corduroy;

I looked in vain
for elbows and wrists;
I counted
the thirty segments, with which

it had rippled its mouse-like dance
over the sea's black floor—not on
feet, which it did not have, but on
tiny buds tipped with bristles,

like paintbrushes—
to find and swallow
the least pulse, and so stay alive, and feel—
however a worm feels it—satisfaction.

Before me
the sea still heaved, and the heavens were dark,
the storm unfinished,
and whatever was still alive

stirred in the awful cup of its power,
though it breathe like fire, though it love
the lung of its own life.
Little mat, little blot, little crawler,

it lay in my hand
all delicate and revolting.
With the tip of my finger
I stroked it,

tenderly, little darling, little dancer,
little pilgrim,
gray pouch slowly
filling with death.

William

Now there's William. He comes pecking, like a bird, at my heart. His eyebrows are like the feathers of a wren. His ears are little seashells.

I would keep him always in my mind's eye.

Soon enough he'll be tall, walking and conversing; he'll have ideas, and a capricious will; the passions will unfold in him, like greased wheels, and he will leap forward upon them.

Who knows, maybe he'll be an athlete, quick and luminous; or a musician, bent like a long-legged pin over the piano's open wing; or maybe he will stand day after day over a drafts-man's desk, making something exquisite and useful—a tower or a bridge.

Whatever he does, he'll want the world to do it in. Maybe, who knows, he'll want this very room which, only for convenience, I realize, I've been calling mine.

I feel myself begin to wilt, like an old flower, weak in the stem.

But he is irresistible! Whatever he wants of mine—my room, my ideas, my glass of milk, my socks and shirts, my place in line, my portion, my world—he may have it.

Early Morning, New Hampshire

Near Wolfeboro,
near the vast, sparkling lake,
deep in the woods,
I swing

my legs over
the old wall and sit
on the iron-cold
stones. The wall

is longer
than any living thing, and quieter
than anything
that breathes, as we

understand breathing. It turns,
it cuts back, it approaches again.
It knows
all the angles.

Somebody
raised it
stone by stone, each lagging weight
pulling the shoulders.

Somebody
meant to sheet these green hills
with domesticity,
and did, for a while.

But not anymore.
And now the unmaking
has, naturally, begun.
Stones fall—

tilt and fall—
but slowly—
only a few a year—
into the leaves, or roll

down into the creeks, or into
the sappy knees
of the pines.
The birds

sing their endless
small alphabets.
Sometimes
a porcupine

hauls itself up and over—
or a deer
makes light of all of it,
leaping and leaping.

But mostly
nothing seems to be happening—
borders and divisions,
old sheep-holders,

the stones just sit there,
mute and tight, and wait
for the instant, gray and wild.
This morning

something slips,
and I see it all—the yearning,
then the blunt and paunchy flight,
then the sweet, dark falling.

Wings

My dog came through the pinewoods dragging a dead fox—
ribs and a spine, and a tail with the fur still on it. Where did
you find this? I said to her, and she showed me. And there
was the skull, there were the leg bones and the shoulder
blades.

I took them home. I scrubbed them and put them on a shelf
to look at—the pelvis, and the snowy helmet. Sometimes, in
the pines, in the starlight, an owl hunches in the dense needles,
and coughs up his pellet—the vole or the mouse recently
eaten. The pellets fall through the branches, through the hair
of the grass. Dark flowers of fur, with a salt of bones and
teeth, melting away.

In Washington, inside the building of glass and stone, and
down the long aisles, and deep inside the drawers, are the
bones of women and children, the bones of old warriors.
Whole skeletons and parts of skeletons. They can't move.
They can't even shiver. Mute, *catalogued*—they lie in the wide
drawers.

So it didn't take long. I could see how it was, and where I
was headed. I took what was left of the fox back to the
pinewoods and buried it. I don't even remember where. I do
remember, though, how I felt. If I had wings I would have
opened them. I would have risen from the ground.

March

There isn't anything in this world but mad love. Not in this
world. No tame love, calm love, mild love, no so-so love.
And, of course, no reasonable love. Also there are a hundred
paths through the world that are easier than loving. But, who
wants easier? We dream of love, we moon about, thinking
of Romeo and Juliet, or Tristan, or the lost queen rushing
away over the Irish sea, all doom and splendor. Today,
on the beach, an old man was sitting in the sun. I called out
to him, and he turned. His face was like an empty pot. I re-
member his tall, pale wife; she died long ago. I remember his
daughter-in-law. When she died, hard, and too young, he
wept in the streets. He picked up pieces of wood, and stones,
and anything else that was there, and threw them at the sea.
Oh, how he loved his wife. Oh, how he loved young Barbara.
I stood in front of him, not expecting any answer yet not
wanting to pass without some greeting. But his face had gone
back to whatever he was dreaming. Something touched me,
lightly, like a knife-blade. I felt I was bleeding, though just
a little, a hint. Inside I flared hot, then cold. I thought of
you. Whom I love, madly.

I Looked Up

I looked up and there it was
among the green branches of the pitchpines—

thick bird,
a ruffle of fire trailing over the shoulders and down the back—

color of copper, iron, bronze—
lighting up the dark branches of the pine.

What misery to be afraid of death.
What wretchedness, to believe only in what can be proven.

When I made a little sound
it looked at me, then it looked past me.

Then it rose, the wings enormous and opulent,
and, as I said, wreathed in fire.

White Pine

The sun rises late in this southern county. And, since the first thing I do when I wake up is go out into the world, I walk here along a dark road. There are many trees. Also, shrubs and vines—sumac, the ivies, honeysuckle. I walk between two green and leafy walls.

Occasionally a rabbit leaps across the road, or a band of deer, tossing their heads and bounding great distances. Maybe some of them leap from the earth altogether. Couldn't there be pastures beside the lakes of the stars? Isn't everything, in the dark, too wonderful to be exact, and circumscribed?

For instance, the white pine that stands by the lake. Tall and dense, it's a whistling crest on windy mornings. Otherwise, it's silent. It looks over the lake and it looks up the road. I don't mean it has eyes. It has long bunches of needles, five to each bundle. From its crown springs a fragrance, the air is sharp with it. Everything is in it. But no single part can be separated from another.

I have read that, in Africa, when the body of an antelope, which all its life ate only leaves and grass and drank nothing but wild water, is first opened, the fragrance is almost too sweet, too delicate, too beautiful to be borne. It is a moment which hunters must pass through carefully, with concentrated and even religious attention, if they are to reach the other side, and go on with their individual lives.

And now I have finished my walk. And I am just standing, quietly, in the darkness, under the tree.

My thanks to the editors of the following magazines, in which poems from the first section of this book have previously appeared:

Appalachia ("Climbing Pinnacle," "White Heron Rises Over Blackwater"), *Cape Cod Voice* ("The Measure," "Truro, the Blueberry Fields"), *Cybernetics and Human Knowing* ("What Is There Beyond Knowing"), *Five Points* ("Honey Locust," "Percy [One]," "Reckless Poem"), *The New Yorker* ("The Poet With His Face in His Hands"), *Onearth* ("Mountain Lion on East Hill Road, Austerlitz, N.Y."), *Orion* ("Lead"), *Poetry* ("The Real Prayers Are Not the Words, but the Attention that Comes First," "Song for Autumn"), *Southern Review* ("Children, It's Spring"), *Spiritus* ("Tiger Lilies," "North Country").